AF566473

Cocurricular Activities:
Their Values and Benefits

Academic Societies and Competitions
Striving for Excellence

Career Preparation Clubs
Goal Oriented

Community Service
Lending a Hand

Foreign Language Clubs
Discovering Other Cultures

Hobby Clubs
Sharing Your Interests

Intramural Sports
Joining the Team

School Publications
Adventures in Media

Science and Technology Clubs
Ideas and Inventions

Student Government and Class Activities
Leaders of Tomorrow

Theater, Speech, and Dance
Expressing Your Talents

Vocal and Instrumental Groups
Making Music

Cocurricular Activities:
Their Values and Benefits

Hobby Clubs

Sharing Your Interests

Betty Bolté

Mason Crest Publishers
Philadelphia

Mason Crest Publishers, Inc.
370 Reed Road
Broomall, PA 19008
(866) MCP-BOOK (toll free)
www.masoncrest.com

First printing

1 2 3 4 5 6 7 8 9 10

Library of Congress Cataloging-in-Publication Data

Bolté, Betty.
Hobby clubs: sharing your interests/by Betty Bolte.
p. cm.—(Cocurricular activities)
ISBN 1-59084-892-6
1. Student activities. 2. Students—Societies and clubs. I. Title. II. Series.
LB3607.B65 2005
371.83—dc22
2004015661

Produced by
Choptank Syndicate, Inc. and Chestnut Productions, L.L.C.
260 Upper Moss Hill Road
Russell, Massachusetts 01071

Project Editors Norman Macht and Mary Hull
Design and Production Lisa Hochstein
Picture Research Mary Hull

OPPOSITE TITLE PAGE
High School student Patricia Homma was named the best teen chef in America at The Art Institutes National Culinary Cook-Off competition.

Table of Contents

Introduction

COCURRICULAR ACTIVITIES BUILD CHARACTER

Sharon L. Ransom
Chief Officer of the Office of Standards-Based Instruction for Chicago Public Schools

Cocurricular activities provide an assortment of athletic, musical, cultural, dramatic, club, and service activities. They provide opportunities based on different talents and interests for students to find their niche while developing character. Character is who we really are. It's what we say and how we say it, what we think, what we value, and how we conduct ourselves in difficult situations. It is character that often determines our success in life and cocurricular activities play a significant role in the development of character in young men and women.

Cocurricular programs and activities provide opportunities to channel the interests and talents of students into positive efforts for the betterment of themselves and the community as a whole. Students who participate in cocurricular activities are often expected to follow certain rules and regulations that prepare them for challenges as well as opportunities later in life.

Many qualities that build character are often taught and nurtured through participation in cocurricular activities. A student learns to make commitments and stick with them through victories and losses as well as achievements and disappointments. They can also learn to build relationships and work collaboratively with others, set goals, and follow the principles and rules of the discipline, club, activity, or sport in which they participate.

Students who are active in cocurricular activities are often successful in school because the traits and behaviors they learn outside of the classroom are important in acquiring and maintaining their academic success. Students become committed to their studies and set academic goals that lead them to triumph. When they relate behaviors, such as following rules or directions or teaming with others, to the classroom, this can result in improved academic achievement.

Students who participate in cocurricular activities and acquire these character-rich behaviors and traits are not likely to be involved in negative behaviors. Peer pressure and negative influences are not as strong for these students, and they are not likely to be involved with drugs, alcohol, or tobacco use. They also attend school more regularly and are less likely to drop out of school.

Students involved in cocurricular activities often are coached or mentored by successful and ethical adults of good and strong character who serve as role models and assist students in setting their goals for the future. These students are also more likely to graduate from high school and go on to college because of their involvement in cocurricular activities.

In this series you will come to realize the many benefits of cocurricular activities. These activities bring success and benefits to individual students, the school, and the community.

Art clubs are one of the most popular school clubs. They offer students the chance to focus on media that interests them, visit museums and galleries, and meet with local artists.

1

Po Hi Art Club

Imagine your school week consisting of only science, math, social studies, and physical education, with a bit of vocabulary and literature thrown in. Would you enjoy it? Classes in the visual and audio arts help make your school days less tedious, and these classes help you to learn your other subjects more easily. Your school most likely has several classes for the different kinds of arts, perhaps orchestra, band, home economics, woodworking, and visual art. Each of these arts can lead to a related school club, like a woodworking club or sewing club.

The art students at one midwestern high school are lucky to have an art teacher who started a club for their enjoyment.

After school, the fifteen members of the art club at Oklahoma's Ponca City High School (Po Hi) troop into the sunny art room, its familiar brightness welcoming the eager young artists. The students take their places at the tables set up alongside many easels, and begin discussing what

Creating painted or silkscreened T-shirts to sell is one way to raise funds for your art club.

they plan to do. One big topic is the upcoming dance fundraiser they're holding at a local youth center. They plan to have several sponsors for the event. Student bands will provide music, and the youth center is providing snacks. A discussion on how to decorate the dance hall takes up some of the meeting time. The money they raise from dance ticket sales will help pay for field trips to local museums, restaurants, and, if all goes well, a trip across the country to New York City.

The art club didn't even exist a few years ago. Then a chance conversation with another teacher prompted Tim Wehrle to begin the club. He wanted to share his love of art with the students on a more one-on-one level and help them experience a more wide-reaching love of all things artistic. He plans to show them an array of art media, beyond what they are likely to experience at home, to broaden their understanding, appreciation, and hopefully love, of art.

The club has been very active. They've traveled to the Gilcrease Museum in Tulsa, where Mr. Wehrle said they would like to return. They marveled at the many examples of western art housed at the museum. The club has also sold popcorn at an art show. One highlight of the club's activities was when the entire art club entered collages in a collage contest sponsored by a local restaurant.

Scholarships for Art Students

If you are serious about art and want to study art at college, you may want to apply for a scholarship from The Art Institutes, the leading educator of students in the creative and applied arts, including design, media, fashion, and culinary programs. There are thirty-one Art Institutes in North America. High school seniors who are members of the National Art Honor Society (NAHS) are eligible for an Art Institute National Art Honor Society Scholarship. Awards are granted based on the quality of the artwork submitted. The NAHS was created in 1978 by the National Art Education Association for high school students in grades ten to twelve to inspire and recognize those with outstanding talent in art. These tuition scholarships range from $25,000 for first prize to $2,500 for fifth. The Art Institutes also offer many other types of scholarships. For more information, contact:

The Art Institutes Admission Department
Free Market Center
210 Sixth Avenue, 32nd Floor
Pittsburgh, PA 15222-2598
1-888-624-0300
www.artinstitutes.edu

The design class held a competition in which students designed bumper stickers and T-shirts to be used for fund-raising. The winners were then sold to the Band Parents group. The club has also been experimenting with silk screen printing and other art forms.

These art club members have seen and tried a wide variety of art styles. Mr. Wehrle is obviously working toward his goals of helping them experience the many different

Creative Arts Contests

If you're looking for a contest you can enter, check out these possibilities:

KinderArt
c/o Jarea Art Studio
Attn: Andrea Mulder-Slater or
Jantje Blokhuis-Mulder
157 Water Street,
St. Andrews, NB
E5B 1A7 Canada
www.kinderart.com

***Teen Ink* magazine**
Box 30
Newton, MA 02461
ph: (617) 964-6800
www.teenink.com

***Writer's Digest* magazine**
4700 E. Galbraith Road
Cincinnati, OH 45236
www.writersdigest.com/contests

National Scholastic Press Association
Associated Collegiate Press
2221 University Avenue SE, Suite 121
Minneapolis, MN 55414
ph: (612) 625-8335
www.studentpress.org/nspa/contests.html

Art clubs enrich the educational experience and give students a chance to find the art within them.

kinds of art. Screenprinting. Western art, including paintings and sculptures of Native Americans and horses. Bumper sticker design. Collages. What will be next? That depends on what the students want to see, and what Mr. Wehrle wants to show them.

Membership is open to any student who has an interest in art. One of Mr. Wehrle's tasks is to keep small groups from forming within the club. "They tend to group up and gossip. We have to keep them on track a lot, yet try to keep it fun."

Although the group is a new addition at the school, the students are glad they have the opportunity to explore different art media and to see what other artists do. They plan to invite several artists to visit and share with them their work and lifestyle.

Art speaks to the members of the Po Hi club. Each member brings a unique vision and point of view to share with the others. Through discussions and a sharing of these differences, each member has a chance to see through different eyes, if only for a brief moment.

The members also enjoy talking about the world of art, and about school, as they work on their projects or discuss plans. Some members are beginning to think about college, and Mr. Wehrle hopes some of them will go on to study art as one club student is already doing at the Chicago Art Institute.

The Po Hi Art Club is off to a great start. The members and advisor are working together to keep the club interesting so that more students will want to be a part of the fun as well as benefit from the art education they receive through the many activities they have planned. They are working together to raise the money to go to New York City, where they hope to visit museums and galleries, broaden their minds, and enjoy being together.

Art clubs are unique in the world of school clubs, as they can help other clubs within the school. Perhaps the Po Hi Art Club will decorate the school for Homecoming, creating posters and signs around the school. Or perhaps they'll volunteer to paint murals on the walls of their school cafeteria or a neighboring elementary school's cafeteria. Maybe they'll aim higher and offer to create a beautiful scenic mural at a senior center or nursing home for local senior citizens to enjoy.

Naturally, they may have to raise money to pay for the paint or other art supplies they'll need to accomplish any of these goals. Car washes, food sales, and other popular moneymakers may need to be explored. Raising money isn't all work—the club members usually have a great time working together. You can read more about some ways your club can raise money in Chapter Four.

No matter what the art club chooses to do, they'll most likely have a good time doing it because they are creating art—something each member loves to do.

Jenny Kwitkowski of Erie, Pennsylvania, holds her winning recipe "Grandmother's Country Chicken Cheddar Casserole." She was the national winner of a Stouffer's "Real Home Cooking" recipe contest.

2

Types of Hobby Clubs

Hobby clubs come in all shapes and sizes, and touch on just about every interest a student could have. The cool thing about hobby clubs is that you get to have fun with your friends while doing something you already enjoy or something you'd like to try. Have you always wanted to try quilting? Or flying a model airplane? Or maybe make a beautiful cedar chest to give to your mother for Christmas? You'll likely either find a club that will meet that interest, or you can see about starting one. Here are a few ideas for some of the more popular clubs that you might find at your school:

ART

Art clubs are one of the most popular clubs in America, and many schools have an art club for those interested in art in all its forms. Members enjoy trips to art exhibits, museums, and sculpture gardens. They are also called upon to decorate the school for special events, like dances,

Homecoming, spirit week, and graduation. There are many art contests and scholarships available for students.

PHOTOGRAPHY

In photography or camera clubs, you can learn to take and develop traditional photos or instantly capture scenes with digital technology. In a photography club, you can learn about not only composition of the picture, but also how to develop film in a dark room. You may even want to experiment with page layouts when you print either traditional photos or digital photos. Clubs take trips to view photography exhibits and learn how to improve skills. Your photography club can go just about anywhere you'd like

Hobby clubs bring people with the same interests together. If you enjoy photography, for example, you will likely benefit from an association with others who share this hobby.

and call it educational as long as you have your camera with you! A trip to Six Flags becomes an adventure in action photography, for example, if you practice taking pictures of the moving rides and your club members screaming on the roller coaster. Club time can be used to plan trips, or for guest photographers to talk to you about how they take professional photos.

Teen Ink magazine holds monthly photography contests for teens. Local fairs, businesses, and organizations, including state parks, run different kinds of photography contests that your club might want to look into.

The National Scholastic Press Association, in conjunction with the National Press Photographers Association, sponsors a Picture of the Year contest with categories for different types of photos, including news, feature, sports, and fine arts.

CRAFTS

There are many different kinds of crafts projects you can do in an arts and crafts club. You might choose to create painted boxes, covered albums, cloth paintings, holiday decorations and gifts, or work with gimp, create paper sculptures using origami techniques, decorate eggs, make cloth flowers, picture frames, windsocks, beaded key chains, or string art pictures. Some clubs combine arts and crafts with sewing. That's what makes this club so much fun—you choose what you want to try to make and then go ahead and do it.

Craft clubs take field trips to crafts stores, fairs, and exhibits. Many crafts stores run classes or seminars that your club may want to attend together.

Your club may want to make some small craft items to sell, or to give to a nursing home or pediatric ward at a

Some crafts clubs make items to sell in order to raise funds for field trips and supplies.

local hospital. Half the fun of making something is giving it to someone who will appreciate it.

SCRAPBOOKING

What do you do with all the photos, ticket stubs, ID cards, and brochures lying around the house? Try incorporating them into scrapbooks, a fun and creative way of showcasing what you've done in your life. Keeping a scrapbook has grown beyond merely sticking papers and photos into an album. Now you can decorate the pages with stickers, cut out shapes, curvy lines, and much more. You'll learn about die cuts, trimmers, borders, and journaling. A lot of the fun comes from sharing the process of making the album, talking about different ways to lay out the photos and stubs, ribbons and brochures, or postcards from your school activities, your vacations with your parents, even day-to-day life.

Most of the cutting tools are not sharp (rounded-nose plastic scissors, paper cutters that use a wire rather than a blade, and corner punches that trim your paper and photo corners into curves) so you should be able to do this at school without any problems. If not, then you might want to share your finished pages and books at your club meetings, or hold the meetings at a member's house or the public library, or even at a local scrapbooking store. No matter where you meet, sharing your creativity with your friends as you share something about your life will make this club something you look forward to attending.

Scrapbooking has exploded in popularity in recent years. These pages were all winners of the "Best Scrapbook Page" contest sponsored by Neenah Paper.

Scrapbooking Resources

Creative Xpress!!
295 West Center Street
Provo, UT 84601
ph: (801) 373-6838
www.creativexpress.com
Offers a monthly contest for original, unpublished scrapbook page layouts.

***Creating Keepsakes* magazine**
14901 Heritagecrest Way
Bluffdale, UT 84065
ph: (888) 247-5282
www.creatingkeepsakes.com
Along with information on scrapbooking, this magazine also sponsors several contests.

***Memory Makers* magazine**
12365 Huron Street, Suite 500
Denver, CO 80234-3438
ph: (386) 246-3404
www.memorymakersmagazine.com
Offers project and page ideas, a place to buy books on scrapbooking, links to other sites, and a list of upcoming scrapbooking events.

Several companies offer layout contests you can enter for fun and prizes. You might also have contests among your club members to see who can design the prettiest page or the most innovative or creative page.

TEXTILE ARTS

Sewing clubs come in many shapes and sizes. The club may want to focus on sewing with a machine, doing embroidery, straight stitching to make clothing, or on handstitching, like cross-stitch, embroidery, or needlepoint.

Knowing how to sew and decorate clothing is a skill that you can do for fun or money.

Do you enjoy crocheting? Your club can make many things with crochet that are easy and fun to do. On their Web site, the Crochet Guild of America posts contests you can enter for the best socks, booties, crochet patterns, and more.

Quilting is another traditional form of sewing. Many people enjoy the beautiful, colorful patterns used to create quilts and quilted wall hangings. In quilting books or at

Textile Arts Resources on the Web

American Sewing Guild
National Headquarters
9660 Hillcroft
Suite 510
Houston, TX 77096
ph: (713) 729-3000
www.asg.org

American Quilter's Society
P.O. Box 3290
Paducah, KY 42002-3290
(800) 626-5420
www.aqsquilt.com

***Rug Hooking* magazine**
1300 Market Street
Suite 202
Lemoyne, PA 17043
(800) 233-9055
www.rughookingonline.com

Crochet Guild of America
P.O. Box 3388
Zanesville, OH 43702-3388
(740) 452-4541
www.crochet.org

quilting Web sites you will find patterns for many different quilting projects.

Rug hooking is a way of creating wall hangings and rugs using short pieces of yarn that are looped, or hooked, through an open-weave cloth such as burlap or linen. Rug hooking kits are available at most crafts stores and through needlework catalogs.

Cloth is made from weaving threads into a pattern. While most people don't think about how their clothes are made, if you'd like to experiment with making cloth from thread, or even make your own thread, then this craft is for you. You'll need a loom, and shuttles to create cloth, and an advisor who knows something about weaving.

No matter which kind of sewing you enjoy, there are ways you can use your talents and skills to help others with your projects. Perhaps you'd enjoy crocheting baby hats and blankets to donate to the pediatric ward at the local hospital. Or you might prefer to make lap quilts to donate to a nursing home for the patients' warmth and comfort. Look around your community and see what you can do to help out.

COOKING

Cooking clubs range from baking cookies to making international foods. Many cooking clubs hold contests within the club for the best recipe in a given category. Some popular categories include cookies, snacks, and sandwiches.

One cooking club holds a monthly contest, with up to five groups of two to five students who develop a recipe. The finished product is then judged by school staff, based on flavor, appearance, and how easy it is to make. First and second place winners of the monthly contests then

Michigan's East Middle School Cooking Club gathers for a picture at the end of a Bake-Off dessert competition. The winners wear chef hats and hold their kitchen utensil trophies.

compete in a second round against each other and any other teams that wish to try. The overall winners are then given a prize—a trip to a nearby student-run school café. Your club can make up its own version of a monthly contest and share the judging with the school. School staff or students will certainly enjoy tasting the club's creations.

Some cooking clubs visit different restaurants and try to guess what seasonings they put in their entrées. Others create new recipes.

Maybe you or your club would like to try entering a recipe contest. Sargento Cheese is always looking for new, tasty ways for consumers to enjoy their cheeses. Enter a favorite recipe with them and you could win $100. The Pillsbury Company holds a yearly bake-off competition with prizes ranging from a $1 million grand prize down to $5,000 for the runner-up. You must be at least thirteen years old and a U.S. resident to enter.

Cooking is a great skill to learn and one you can practice for a lifetime. It also provides an opportunity to showcase your individual tastes and preferences in an artistic way.

Your favorite family entrée or casserole recipe could end up as a Stouffer's Family Style Favorites frozen entrée if you enter it in the Stouffer's Real Home Cooking contest, where main dish entries are judged on the basis of broad family appeal, their adaptability to frozen food production, and the history and tradition of the recipe. Each recipe must include a written paragraph of one hundred fifty words or less describing the dish's origin, when you serve it, and what it means to you or your family. The winner receives $10,000 and their recipe becomes a Stouffer's frozen entrée.

If you enjoy cooking and creating and are thinking about becoming a professional chef when you finish high school,

A teen chef competes in The Art Institutes National Culinary Cook-Off competition.

you can apply for an Art Institutes Culinary Scholarship. You must be a high school senior to win a full- or partial-tuition scholarship to one of the Art Institutes that offer a Culinary Arts program.

The National Restaurant Association offers the ProStart Program, designed to help young people explore careers in the restaurant and food service industry. You can earn a national Certificate of Achievement, set up an internship with a restaurant, caterer, or other food service business, or compete for several college scholarships ranging from $2,000 to $5,000.

Cooking Contests

Want to test your cooking skills? Try out one of these contests:

Sargento Foods, Inc.
One Persnickety Place
Plymouth, WA 53073
ph: (800) CHEESES
www.sargentocheese.com/recipe/contest.jsp

Pillsbury
General Mills Inc.
Attn: Consumer Services
Number One General Mills Boulevard
Minneapolis, MN 55426
ph: (800) 775-4777
www.pillsbury.com/bakeoff

Stouffers
Nestlé USA
Consumer Services Center
P.O. Box 2178
Wilkes-Barre, PA 18703
ph: (800) 225-1180
www.stouffers.com

MAGIC

Magicians are popular the world over for entertaining and surprising audiences. You can learn and practice traditional tricks like card tricks, nut and shell games, making small objects disappear (such as a quarter vanishing before your eyes), or pulling an object out of an empty space (like a scarf out of an empty fist). You might even make up some of your own tricks to try on your friends. A magic club has a built-in fundraiser—giving performances for local groups or birthday parties to raise money for your club to attend professional magic shows. Clubs travel to nearby magic shops and explore the treasures there.

If you're serious about being a magician, you may want

to join the Magic Youth International organization. This is the youth program of the International Brotherhood of Magicians (the I.B.M.), the "largest magic organization in the world," according to their Web site. The MYI was formed to help promote young magicians. They also publish a magazine, *Top Hat,* which is full of photos and information by other young magicians, as well as tips to make your magic better, special effects, and more. You have to be a member of the I.B.M. to join. Go to their Web site for more information on how to join. You can write to the I.B.M. for an application at: **I.B.M. Application, 11155C South Towne Square, St. Louis, Missouri, 63123**. You will be asked for the names of two I.B.M. members who know you to sponsor your application, or you can send your application to **Magic Youth International, 159 Ralston Avenue, Kenmore, New York, 14217**, and they will find sponsors for you.

CHESS

Many schools have chess clubs, and strategy is the name of this game. Chess skills help you to learn how to plan

Tidbits About Chess

Did You Know...

- chess is played in every country in the world?
- annually, more than 100,000 students learn how to play chess in North America alone?
- chess helps your overall ability to learn in school?
- after two moves by each player, more than 70,000 different moves can be made?

your moves (in chess and in life). Chess games can last a few minutes to several hours, depending on how skilled the players are. Anyone can join who is interested in learning how to play. Many clubs also develop tournaments. Tournaments can be against other schools' chess clubs, or your club can compete in regional and possibly even national tourneys. You can register your club with the U.S. Chess Federation and receive newsletters and information from them.

GAMES CLUBS

Students who like playing Monopoly or Parchesi, or any or all other board games, often form a game club to hone their skills and enjoy the competition with fellow enthusiasts.

SCRABBLE®. This board game is fun and tests your vocabulary skills. You will not only use the words you know, you'll also learn new ones and improve your spelling, dictionary, math, conflict resolution, and creative problem solving skills. More than one million students in 20,000 American schools play Scrabble. The National Scrabble Association started the National School Scrabble Program in 1991. They have information on Scrabble clubs and tournaments at their Web site. You must be in grades five through eight to compete in the national tournaments; most years they have a waiting list of competitors.

Trivial Pursuit®. This board game is a question and answer trivia game with several different editions. Up to six players can play at one time. Each player is given a game piece with six pie-shaped openings in it. You move around the board answering questions. When you are on a pie-shaped place on the board and answer the question right, then you earn a pie piece. It's fun to test your knowledge

Scrabble is one of the most popular board games ever invented. Each year Scrabble enthusiasts enter the National and World Scrabble Championships.

about the little things in life, to see how observant you are, and to learn some new facts.

Some people make up their own trivia games, based on this concept, to help quiz each other on a specific topic, such as soccer rules, history, or horse management.

Role Playing Games. Have you heard of Dungeons and Dragons? Now you can act out the story for yourself. Role playing games (RPGs) are based on acting out a character in a make-believe story. They are often based on television shows, such as *The Simpsons*, or sci-fi stories like *Buffy the*

Trivia Scavenger Hunt

If you love trivia, you may want to consider this activity that a high school in California uses for an annual friendly competition.

Each February the school hosts a trivia scavenger hunt called the Friends of Millard Fillmore Trivia Hunt. With the help of parents, students search for the answers to questions, such as "find the name of the first female to play on the Harlem Globetrotters."

But there's a twist: each answer must be backed up by documentation, proof the answer is correct. At the end of the forty-eight-hour hunt for facts, the answers are judged. Each team of scavengers elects a reader (who will read their answers to the judging panel) and a lawyer (who will defend their answers).

Being the lawyer for a team requires self-confidence, and a good understanding of the material. The lawyer needs to know when to defend an answer and when to realize that an answer isn't correct. Teamwork is at the core of success. Teams have been as large as twenty students who work on the questions over a weekend, with the final judging on Sunday evening.

Vampire Slayer or *StarGate–SG1*, or medieval stories like *Greyhawk Adventures* and *DragonLance*. Club meetings usually last several hours to allow time to play the games.

Basically, each club member plays a part in the story, acting and reacting as the character. Some games require you to create a character. Either way, you become the character and make choices on how that character would respond to dangers, like aliens shooting at you, or a vampire attacking, or maybe a secret door that you stumble upon. RPGs are also played at events in many cities around the world.

As you progress into the role playing game, you may

need to purchase rulebooks and a set of multifaceted dice, but to start you simply need a notebook, a pencil, and you. You may even want to dress the part by making or purchasing costumes.

You can join the national organization for role playing, called the Role Playing Gamers' Association (RPGA). Their Web site is crammed full of information on many different games, how to become a member, an events calendar, and much more. To join the RPGA, with a free, lifetime membership, you must attend an event and fill out a membership application. The Games Master (GM) will give you a membership card at that time, and you can begin playing. Your club can become a sanctioned role playing club by the RPGA and host its own events.

WRITING AND READING

These clubs include ones that focus on reading, poetry, fiction writing, and scriptwriting. You'll also find people who may be interested in creating a literary magazine, or writing for a newspaper, or who just want to read and discuss good books.

Writing fiction is different from writing an essay for school. With fiction, or creative writing, you choose what world your characters exist in, what they want out of life, and whether they achieve their goals. Scriptwriting focuses on writing plays and movie scripts.

Journalists write for newspapers and magazines. Many schools have a school newspaper or a literary magazine. Each lets you write in a different style with a different focus. You can have fun learning how to lay out a newspaper, check its accuracy, and then share it with fellow students. The school literary magazine is usually full of stories, essays, articles, art work, poems, and other items related to literature. Field trips might include a visit to a local newspaper or magazine publisher to learn about how they run their businesses, or to speak to a local magazine journalist.

There are many writing contests you can enter, including one for youth that is sponsored by *Writer's Digest* magazine. You must be thirteen years old or younger to enter the "Your Assignment for Kids" contest. Each month, *Writer's Digest* posts a topic (like "Cookie Surprise" or "Can You Haiku?") that you have to write about within the given word count. You can win a free copy of *The Young Writer's Guide to Getting Published*, plus a certificate of achievement, a copy of the latest issue of *Writer's Digest* magazine, and a $10 gift certificate to the bookstore Barnes and Noble. No matter which form of creative writing you enjoy, this type of club is all about sharing your creative insight into the world around you. Making up stories to tell others for their pleasure is an age-old way of passing on knowledge, experience, and fun.

Teen Ink magazine runs contests, including ones for fiction and poetry. They have a long list of other contests at their Web site. *Stone Soup* is another magazine for young writers and artists who are eight to thirteen years old. All the material in the magazine is written or created by young artists

Reading or literary clubs are discussion groups for current and classic fiction or nonfiction books. It's fun to share with others your thoughts about the story line, the writing, the setting, and even the words selected by the author. You may want to find out about the author's life and other works. Book clubs exist all over the country, in bookstores, libraries, and other places where readers and writers gather. Why not in your school?

There are kits available to help you assemble models of all kinds from planes to rockets.

MODEL CLUBS

Rockets, airplanes, cars, trains—if you love to build models, these are some of the most common models that school clubs build.

Rockets and airplanes are fun to build and decorate. Some models snap together, others are glued. Some come with stickers to put on, others need paint. Model rockets are usually sold in kits at hobby or craft stores. Many people of all ages enjoy putting together model rockets or airplanes so they can then launch them in a big, open field to see how high they will fly. Some model airplanes have remote controls to control their maneuvers.

Car models also come in kits, from the first Fords, Model A and Model T, to today's Chevy Corvette. If you love cars and working with your hands, this club may be fun.

Model trains are loved by everyone. They are fun to work

with, and builders often design little towns for the train to run around on its tracks. You can create a miniature town—perhaps your own hometown, or one from your imagination. Hobby stores sell many small trees, animals, fences, houses, cars, lamp posts, and fire hydrants that you can use to build the setting for your train. You can also use your artistic talents and build, paint, and otherwise create your landscape and town.

Do you enjoy building some other kind of model? Perhaps you can find some friends who'd like to form a new model club.

AMATEUR RADIO

People of all ages have used amateur radios for more than ninety years to talk, share information, and warn of emergencies or traffic conditions. Becoming a ham radio operator (someone who uses an amateur radio) is a simple process. Once you obtain a valid license, you can talk on specific radio bands and design, build, modify, and repair your own equipment.

Two major organizations are responsible for emergency communication. The Amateur Radio Emergency Service (ARES) is a public service group led by the American Radio Relay League (ARRL) to coordinate volunteer ham operators to help during natural disasters and for major public events like marathons and road races. The second group, SKYWARN, is sponsored by the National Weather Service to report dangerous weather conditions.

There are local and national organizations associated with ham operators. The ARRL offers several courses in ham radio operation, including antenna modeling and introduction to ARES. The ARRL offers several scholarships for amounts from $1,000 to $10,000 per year. You can plan

A student amateur radio operator makes contact over the airwaves. Amateur radio enthusiasts enjoy trying to make contact in different parts of the world.

to study in any of several areas to receive the scholarship: computers, medicine, engineering, or communications.

ASTRONOMY

Star gazing brings about a sense of awe in most people. How far away are the stars and the planets? Astronomy clubs help you develop a greater understanding of the stars in the sky. You can learn about constellations, star names, and where planets are during the different seasons. Explore the history and stories behind the stars and their constellations. Special equipment is used to study stars, such as telescopes, cameras, and computer programs. Maybe you can visit an observatory to view special astronomical events. A simple telescope out in someone's back yard can be fun to share.

Many observatories and universities offer astronomy clubs and programs. Some observatories allow patrons to use their smaller telescopes.

HISTORY

Even if history is not your favorite class, you might discover that history clubs can be fun. History clubs make it possible to explore history from many angles that classroom time doesn't allow. You will learn more about research techniques and methods, such as how to locate primary sources rather than secondary sources, and how to verify their accuracy. Field trips can be arranged to visit local battlefields and historical sites, or state museums and libraries where history surrounds you. A trip to a historical site, such as an old mill or early home, in your town or city can be fascinating when you know the story behind the site.

Each year the National History Day (NHD) competition

Army ROTC Cadet Kristopher Cottle created a history club at his school, Olympic High in Charlotte, North Carolina, not just because he was interested in the subject, but as a way to tutor other students.

takes place across the country. The NHD organization is a nonprofit group located at the University of Maryland. Students in grades six through twelve are eligible to compete. Student groups research and develop a performance, documentary, or educational exhibit based on that year's contest theme. Individual students can also write a research paper to enter. Projects compete at the regional level first. Winners at the regional level go on to the national competition. Projects are judged on historical quality, presentation, and how well the project sticks to the annual theme. Prizes at the national competition are awarded for the first three places. First place receives $1,000, second place $500, and third place $250. Other prizes are awarded in certain special categories.

The National History Club

The National History Club encourages the reading, writing, discussion, and enjoyment of foreign and domestic, ancient and modern history. Members gather to share ideas and experiences and promote an interest in history.

Today, over 1,700 students in secondary schools in 26 states are involved in the National History Club. The club publishes a newsletter twice a year that is available at its Web site. The newsletter gives information about club activities from chapters around the country.

What kinds of activities might you experience? Some History Clubs focus on local history and visit historical sites in their area. Other clubs sponsor History Fairs or History Days. Some groups read history books together that they discuss. Some clubs read books and then write papers about historical subjects.

If you love history and want to join others who share your enthusiasm, consider starting a history club in your school. Contact **<www.tcr.org/nhc.html>** for more information.

GENEALOGY

Knowing where your family comes from and who they were can help you know more about yourself. You've probably created a family tree in one of your classes, usually in elementary school. But there's more to know about your family than just your parents and grandparents. Were they merchants, farmers, bank robbers? Where did they come from—England, China, Ireland, Egypt?

Genealogy clubs explore history from a family viewpoint. Your history classes, geography classes, and library and research skills will all be useful in this club. You can find out about census records, vital records, probate records, ships' passenger lists, military history records, gravestone rubbings, and how to write a family history. Some amateur genealogists become professional genealogy researchers.

FILM

Cary Grant. Barbara Stanwyck. John Wayne. Do these actors' names make you think of scenes from great classic movies? Maybe you like classic comedies or foreign or indie films. Or maybe you'd prefer to study more recent films, starring Tom Cruise, Madonna, or Jackie Chan. There is something to be enjoyed, shared, or learned from each film genre.

Just like great books, you can watch and discuss films, sharing them with fellow students who enjoy them as well. On field trips you can visit museums or exhibits about classic films. You can hold a viewing where people can watch these movies and buy popcorn from the club.

These are just a few of the many hobby club possibilities you have to choose from at your school. And remember: you can come up with your own club to share your interests (whatever they are) as long as there are other students who want to join. Have fun!

Through meetings, field trips, and fundraisers, you'll get to know your fellow club members and hopefully make lasting friendships.

3

Getting Involved

Now that you've read about some of the choices in school clubs, you may be thinking about your own school. What clubs does your school have? Most middle and high schools have many different clubs, though some schools have very few. It all depends on the interests and commitments of the students and teachers.

Through your club membership you will share a common hobby, make friends, and learn more about working together on a project and sharing information that will help a fellow club member.

School clubs are different from the friends clubs of your preschool and elementary years. Hobby clubs in middle and high school exist to help you make friends, and share a common interest, but they are also there to help you learn how to start, and, more importantly, finish a project. Your club members will help motivate you to complete the project you choose to begin, just as you will help them—all just by being together in a group sharing the fun of your

Students listen intently to a guest speaker at a club meeting. Inviting guest speakers is a great way to enliven monthly meetings and learn more about your hobby.

chosen hobby. You won't even realize that you're learning—you'll be having too much fun to notice.

Clubs usually convene on a regular basis, but how often they meet and where they meet varies by club. Meetings for clubs depend on the schedule at your school, the desires of the club members, and the advisor's availability. Some clubs meet every week, or twice a month, or once a month. What's important is that your club meets as much as the members want to meet. With major projects, you may find your club needs to add meetings, maybe even on weekends.

Meeting time may be used to plan activities and fundraisers, or discuss new techniques or rules for your hobby. Your advisor may have important information to share with you about upcoming seminars or college scholarships that have been made available.

Starting a Hobby Club

What if your interest isn't included in your school's club list? As with any kind of club, you'll need to ask permission from your school principal to start a new club. You'll need an advisor, typically a teacher who shares your interest, and a few friends who would like to have such a club. How do you find these things?

You might start by asking your friends and classmates at school if they want to help you start a club. When you have a group of students who are interested, ask a teacher to be the club's advisor. (Keep in mind that teachers take on school clubs on a volunteer basis, and that every teacher has a life outside of school just like you do.)

Once you have a group of students and an advisor, ask your principal for permission. If you're unsure of how to do this, ask your teacher for guidance. Perhaps your teacher might even go with you to speak to the principal.

Once the principal gives you permission to proceed, you need to let the other students know about the new club forming. Set a date to have a meeting to discuss when you'll meet, how often, and ideas for activities you'd like to do. Decide if you want to have officers, or if your advisor will direct the meetings. Begin to plan how you will meet your goals. Will you need to raise some money to cover expenses? Will club members pay dues or just pitch in whatever is needed as they go?

Be sure to make a list of who attended so you know who to contact for your next meeting. Often, you can ask the school office to announce your next meeting date and time, and you can make some posters to put up around your school.

MEETINGS

During your club's meetings over the course of the school year, you'll find that not only will you make friends within the club, but you'll also know your advisor better, as a person with a common interest. Usually, advisors are teachers who volunteer to supervise and guide the club. This allows the teacher to interact with students on a more personal level, sharing a common interest rather than a forced curriculum.

Your advisor will help you identify guest speakers and presenters, such as dancing groups, musicians, and artists. You might be able to have a representative of a national organization visit your club.

Your hobby club has the ability to connect with state, regional, and national organizations that can provide support and opportunities that are broader than what a typical school can offer. For example, many organizations for amateur radio operators offer college scholarships to licensed ham operators.

Field trips and guest speakers are fun to plan as well as to experience. The club should decide where they want to visit—such as a restaurant, a festival, or an art exhibit—then discuss how they will afford to make the trip. Will the club members pay their own way? Seek donations? Hold a fundraiser?

Your club can choose what it wants to do throughout the year. You will need to make sure that any trips you plan are approved by your advisor and possibly your school principal. Your advisor will be able to help you work out the details for arranging field trips. For example, you need to decide how you will travel (private car, bus, train, plane) and how long you will be gone. If you're going to be gone for more than a day, other travel arrangements will need to be made for lodging, meals, and perhaps tours when you arrive.

So what might you want to do? Members in each club will have their own ideas as to how to spend their time. A brainstorming session may be needed, where everyone can suggest possible projects and trips. Then you can vote on them and decide from the results.

To get you started, here are a few ideas for possible activities that you and your fellow club members can use to jumpstart your own brainstorming session:

- Put on a demonstration of your club's activities at a school assembly or at a community center. You could also do this at a nursing home or daycare center.

Making Your Club Great

The most important thing each club member can do to ensure an active, healthy club is to attend the meetings.

Remember, you are all there to share a common interest. To receive the most reward from your joint efforts, it's important that everyone work together as much as possible.

At your first meeting each year, suggest that everyone introduce themselves. Perhaps they can say something about what they are working on, or how long they've been in the club and why. The goal is to get everyone talking and sharing.

If your advisor is leading the group, be sure you are actively listening, participating, and making suggestions. Keep in mind that this club is for all the members, and that the advisor wants to help you have a great time as you explore this hobby. Ask questions. Make suggestions. Be involved.

If you have club officers, be sure that you present your ideas and listen carefully to what others want to do. Once an agreement is reached, club members should try to work together to accomplish the goal.

If you have trouble working with a student, try to figure out what is causing the problem. If you cannot solve that problem, then talk to your advisor for ideas on how to handle the situation.

- Travel to a museum or exhibit. Many crafts and hobbies have related museums and exhibits, such as the auto and train museum at the Smithsonian Museum in Washington, D.C. If you're into sewing, especially quilting, you may find an exhibit at a prairie or early American town museum, such as Williamsburg, Virginia, or the Conner Prairie Museum in Noblesville, Indiana. History buffs may enjoy a local Renaissance Festival or the U.S. Army Cavalry museum located at Fort Riley, Kansas. A quick Internet search can tell you of other sites close to your school.
- Go to a hobby show. One of the largest in the world is the hobby show held at the International Centre in Mississauga, Ontario, Canada. Over 25,000 visitors from around the world attend each year to see demonstrations, go to workshops and seminars, and view products related to more than 200 different crafts and hobbies—everything from remote controlled planes to kites and pottery. Meeting other hobby enthusiasts is a great way to get new ideas.
- Attend a seminar or workshop on your craft or hobby; scrapbooking, model trains, ham radio, and needlework are just a few examples of hobbies that have these kinds of events.
- Plan a community service project for your club. Perhaps you could make flower arrangements, quilts, or crocheted afghans for a senior center. The club could throw a party for a younger group of children using some aspect of your hobby interest to entertain them, such as a magic show or roleplaying event. Service to your community

might be simply picking up trash along a street, holding a food drive, or collecting cans to recycle.

- Contribute to school spirit by having your club decorate your school for pep rallies or Homecoming activities. Graduation and concert nights are also good chances to help out around the school. Look around your community and see if there isn't some way your club can contribute.

Pitch a ball, hit the target, and burst a water balloon over someone's head. Renting a booth like this for a school carnival or fair is one way to raise funds for your hobby club.

4

Financing Your Fun

Not every club will need to raise money; just collecting dues may cover your costs. But if your club has big plans for a trip or special event, you'll probably have to raise the money outside of your meeting room.

Some fundraisers are hard work, but most are easy. Making it fun lightens the burden for everyone. Start by deciding how much money you need to raise. Think about how much the trip, event, or project will cost. Be sure to include a miscellaneous expense fund for those costs you didn't (or can't) anticipate.

Next, decide who will lead the fundraising effort. Will your advisor do it, or will you form a committee to work together on it? While the entire club will be involved in raising money, it's important that only one or two people lead the group. You'll want someone to lead who knows how to talk to people politely and effectively. Make a list of people who will be on the committee, including phone numbers and e-mail addresses (if they have them). The

Dressing the Part

It's important that you look neat when you ask business people and store owners to contribute to your club's finances.

A nice shirt, clean and neat slacks or jeans, clean shoes, and combed hair create a look that many adults favor in students. Remember that your aim is to convince these people that your club is worth giving money to. Businesses and stores are asked quite often to donate to various charities and groups, and they have to choose carefully which they want to support.

The way you present yourself to them can make or break the donation. If you're unsure what to wear, check with your parents or advisor for guidance.

committee chair will be responsible for calling meetings of the committee and making sure the group is making good progress toward their goals.

Decide on a good fundraising idea that will raise enough money for your needs. Remember that people will donate money to help you reach a goal, but you should only raise as much money as you need for the club's goals. Otherwise, you haven't told the whole truth to your supporters. Of course, if you collect money "for the club" and not for a specific expense, then people will understand that any extra money will be used for other club activities.

You may need to have a pep talk with your club members as some may be hesitant to ask folks for money or to sell items. Also, with so many other groups, in and out of school, trying to raise money, you'll need to think of something creative to do that will catch people's attention. Parents, in particular, are often reluctant to approach their coworkers and friends yet again to ask them to buy Christmas wrap or popcorn. Imagine what you would like to see offered, then determine whether that is a feasible way for your club to raise the desired amount of money

Sometimes it is easier to simply ask for donations of money to cover your expenses. In that case, you'll need to keep careful records. Be sure all checks clear the bank before you actually count on the money as having been received.

You'll also need to discuss ways you can spread the word about the club's money-making endeavors. School announcements, school newsletters, flyers, and posters are all ways you can do this. Depending on the size and complexity of the fundraiser, you might want to ask for free space in the newspaper, or maybe the newspaper would interview someone from the club. Tell your school parent-teacher association and other groups in your school.

As the club sells items and collects money, someone in the club will need to be responsible for keeping track of where the money comes from and how much is collected. Sometimes you'll need to keep track of orders taken and any money that's collected before or after the items are delivered. Other times you will collect the money as you sell the item. Each method has a different tracking requirement. Decide among your club members, with your advisor's help, exactly what and how you will keep track of money collected.

One way to encourage your club members to sell as much as possible is to have prizes you can award at various levels of sales. The levels need to be determined based on how much money your club needs to raise. The prizes can be free ice cream at lunch, or McDonald's coupons, or other small gifts. They don't need to be expensive or elaborate to be effective. Perhaps you want to give each club member who sells his or her quota an item related to your shared hobby, such as a new tool, a subscription to a relevant magazine, or an event ticket. Your advisor can help you set these incentives.

FUNDRAISING IDEAS AND ACTIVITIES

There are basically two kinds of fundraisers: order taking and direct sales. Order taking is a no-cost way of raising money. You've probably already participated in one of these through your school. Potential customers look through a brochure of products, select what they want, pay for it (at the time of order or when delivered), and then receive the products later. This type of fundraiser eliminates the guesswork of how many items to order and lets your customers choose from a wide range of items. On the down side, you have to deliver the products, collect the money, and hope that all the checks clear the bank. If the customer hasn't paid for the item already, they may decide they don't want it when you go to deliver it, and you can't send the product back to the distributor. You're stuck with it.

With direct sales you have one or more products to sell, and you collect the money as you hand over the item to the customer. This way customers can see what you are selling, right there in front of them. Direct sales efforts are also finished in a shorter time than order taking, so you can raise the money for your club quicker. However, it's easy to have more product than customers if you order too much, leaving someone with a garage full of candy, cookies, balloons, or scented candles.

As mentioned earlier, it is better to try to find a new way to sell items and/or ask for money. A creative fundraiser attracts more attention, and thus more customers who are more likely to buy something from your club members. The following is a list of several fundraising ideas other groups

Making cookies or other baked goods to sell during school breaks or at school-sponsored activities is one way to raise funds for your club.

and organizations have used across the country. They are here to give you a starting point to look for new ideas, and to perhaps modify to suit your club's individual interests and strengths. If you need more suggestions, you can find many sources of information on the Internet and in your public library.

Bake sale. The club can bake various goodies and sell them at school dances or during lunch in the cafeteria. Bake sales are popular during athletic events like football or basketball games, too. You can get fancy and put the cookies in pretty bags with bows or other tie-ons, and then charge a little more for the packaging. Or instead of baking goodies for people, try making dog treats and selling them at a pet store or local dog show.

Craft sales. If your club is a sewing or craft club, you might be able to make your own items to sell, such as quilted placemats or bags, knitted or crocheted scarves, homemade beeswax candles, or pretty blank cards. You could even put together "snack attack survival kits" to sell during break or after school.

Pizza sales. Most people enjoy pizza, so what easier way to make money than to have a pizza sale? You can take orders for various kinds of pizza, limiting customers' choices to two or three kinds. Buy the makings for the pizzas (crusts, sauce, toppings) and get together on a Saturday morning to put them together. Arrange a time for people to pick up their pizzas, which will be ready to put in the oven when they get them home.

Personalized Holiday Cookies. Bake cookies in the shape of hearts, eggs, or four-leaf clovers (depending on the closest holiday) and take orders for personalizing them. You can use decorator icing to write messages on the cookies, then deliver them (for an additional fee) on the holiday. This is also a great idea to tailor for school events, such as spirit week or Homecoming.

Breakfast with the Easter Bunny. Hold an Easter breakfast, complete with an egg hunt and the Easter Bunny. Invite local craft stores, boutiques, and other small stores to set up a booth, which you can rent to them for a small fee. Include a booth to display what your club is doing as well. Serve a pancake breakfast, and let parents shop while the kids hunt eggs and visit with the bunny.

Raffle. Raffles are easy ways to make some money if you know what to offer. How about tickets to an upcoming concert, an ATV, or a new bike? Many stores will provide an item at cost for a charity or club to auction or raffle. That means any money the raffle makes above the cost of the item is yours to keep. Your only expenses are printing the tickets and the cost of the prize.

Downhill Ball Race. This is a version of the downstream

Selling Safely

Remember these important tips when you are preparing to sell door-to-door or at an event:

- Never go out after dark to sell products.
- Sell first to people you know—friends, family, and neighbors. Then ask your parents to ask at work. Don't sell or talk to strangers without a parent with you.
- Use the phone or e-mail to contact other people you know about supporting your group.
- Take someone with you, whether it's another club member or a friend or relative.
- Be polite, but do not enter a house where you don't know the people who live there.
- Carry only small amounts of money with you.

duck races. Number donated balls (such as tennis or ping pong balls) and sell chances ($1 each perhaps) on which one will be at the finish line (the bottom of the hill) first. The winner gets half the money or another prize.

Hold a Non-Event. This is a way to raise some money without having to do anything other than send out invitations inviting people to an event that won't happen on a given date and time, won't include refreshments, or a fancy dress or tux, or the need for a babysitter. Then you ask for a donation of a specified amount, since they've saved so much by not attending.

FINDING SPONSORS

Sponsors are people and businesses who donate money or products to help with your group's goals. For example, it might be a donation of pancake mix for a breakfast event, or a donation of cash to purchase flowers at wholesale so you can resell them.

Before asking anyone to donate to your club, make a plan. First, list as many potential sponsors as you can: family members, friends, your parents' friends, neighbors, local businesses, and any others who might be interested in supporting your cause.

Second, write down what you want to say to sponsors when asking for a donation. Know why your club wants the donation. If you are planning a trip and want to raise money to cover expenses, say so: "Our Art club is raising money to attend an exhibit in New York City this fall."

You might write out a greeting to use when you approach people. Everyone gets nervous making "cold calls." Writing it down will help you feel calmer and more prepared. It might read something like this: "Hi, my name is Sue, and the middle school chess club is raising money for an upcoming tournament in Nashville. Would you care to help our group by (donating money or an item)? Thank you very much!"

Remember to smile and use your best manners.

SAYING THANKS

After you've received a promise to provide money or items to your club, it's important that you acknowledge your sponsor's generosity. Many sponsors love to display the thank-you letters, notes, photos, plaques, or gifts that clubs and groups send to them. Those same sponsors are more likely to give to the group again if you thank them for each donation they make.

Saying thanks doesn't have to be boring, either. You can take a photo of your club with the donation, or at the event for which you were raising the money, then send a matted, signed copy of it to the sponsors who helped get you there. Or you can make them a gift—a silk flower arrangement, a crafts project or an art project—and send or deliver it to them. No matter how you say thanks, be sure to do it. A simple thank-you card signed by the club members will bring a smile to your sponsor's face and leave that lasting impression you're looking for. After all, everyone likes to be appreciated, and this is one small way of letting someone know you are grateful for their support.

Glossary

advisor–a person who gives advice to another person or group.

amateur radio–a shortwave two-way radio used to communicate.

donator–a person or business that gives, donates, or presents something.

fundraiser–A social event held to raise money.

game master–the person in charge of role playing games.

ham operator–a person who uses an amateur (ham) radio.

role playing game–a play-acting game in which people pretend to be a character.

scholarship–money given to a student to pay for class tuition and expenses.

sponsor–a person or business who donates money or items to a group or club, usually in exchange for recognition by the club.

Internet

www.aarl.org
The American Radio Relay Web site.

www.kidshamradio.com
Site with useful links for student ham radio operators.

www.artnewsonline.com
The *ARTnews* site has many links to museums, galleries, and events in the arts.

www.pcpphotomag.com
The *PC Photo Magazine* site is dedicated to digital photography.

http://school.scrabble-assoc.com
Web site of the National SCRABBLE® Association.

www.uschess.org
The Web site of the U.S. Chess Federation.

www.familytreemagazine.com
The *Family Tree Magazine* genealogy Web site.

www.nationalhistoryday.org
The National History Day site.

www.magicyouth.com
The Web site of Magic Youth International.

www.rpga.com
The Role Playing Gamer's Association Web site.

www.trains.com
Information for beginning model train enthusiasts.

www.school-fund-raisers.com
This site sells school fundraising products such as candy, candles, and flower bulbs.

Further Reading

Canby, Vincent, et al. *The New York Times Guide to the Best 1,000 Movies Ever Made.* New York: Three Rivers Press, 1999.

Check, Laura. *Almost Instant Scrapbooks.* Charlotte, Vermont: Williamson Publishing, 2003.

Darling, Jennifer Dorland, editor. *Better Homes and Gardens New Junior Cookbook.* Des Moines: Meredith Books, 1997.

Joachim, Jean, and Elizabeth Beir. *Beyond the Bake Sale: The Ultimate School Fund-Raising Book.* New York: St. Martin's Press, 2003.

Snyder, Robert M. *Chess for Juniors: A Complete Guide for the Beginner.* New York: Random House, 1991.

Thibault, Terri, et al. *Kids' Easy Quilting Projects.* Charlotte, Vermont: Williamson Publishing, 2001.

Umnik, Sharon Dunn. *175 Easy-To-Do Everyday Crafts.* Honesdale, Pennsylvania: Boyds Mill Press, 1995.

Wenger, Jennifer, Carol Abrams, and Maureen Lasher. *Teen Knitting Club: Chill Out and Knit Some Cool Stuff.* New York: Artisan, 2004.

Williams, Randal. *Rosen Photo Guide to a Career in Magic.* New York: Rosen Publishing Group, 1988.

Wolfman, Ira. *Climbing Your Family Tree: Online and Off-line Genealogy for Kids.* New York: Workman Publishing Co., 2002.

Wood, Heather. *101 Marvelous Money-Making Ideas for Kids.* New York: Tor Books, 1995.

Index

PICTURE CREDITS

Cover: Benjamin Stewart, Image Source, Banana Stock.
Interior: P. R. News Foto/The Art Institutes, 2, 27; ©Ulrich Tutsch, 8, 13; ©Oscar C. Williams, 10; Feature Photo Service/Stouffers, 16; Photos.com, 18, 20, 26, 35, 38, 42, 55; P. R. News Foto/Neenah Paper, 21; Courtesy of Danielle Kovachevich/East Middle School, Huntington Woods, MI, 25; Wide World Photo/Eric Jamison, 31; Courtesy of St. Aloysius Radio Club, Shepherdsville Kentucky, photo by Buddy Sohl KC4WQ, 37; P. R. News Foto/Luquire George Andrew, 39; P. R. News Foto/Junior Achievement, 44; P.R. News Foto/WhirlWhims, LLC, 50.

ABOUT THE AUTHOR

Betty Bolté is a freelance writer and editor. She has written several books, a monthly newspaper column, and more than fifty general interest articles. Bolté graduated from Indiana University in 1995 with a degree in English and a minor in Anthropology. She lives on a horse farm in Taft, Tennessee, with her husband, two teenagers, and her father.

SERIES CONSULTANT

Series Consultant Sharon L. Ransom is Chief Officer of the Office of Standards-Based Instruction for Chicago Public Schools and Lecturer at the University of Illinois at Chicago. She is the founding director of the Achieving High Standards Project: a Standards-Based Comprehensive School Reform project at the University of Illinois at Chicago, and she is the former director of the Partnership READ Project: a Standards Based Change Process. Her work has included school reform issues that center on literacy instruction, as well as developing standards-based curriculum and assessments, improving school leadership, and promoting school, parent, and community partnerships. In 1999, she received the Martin Luther King Outstanding Educator's Award.